Anonymous

Buckle's Stables, Out Buildings and Fences

Anonymous

Buckle's Stables, Out Buildings and Fences

ISBN/EAN: 9783337321031

Printed in Europe, USA, Canada, Australia, Japan

Cover: Foto ©ninafisch / pixelio.de

More available books at **www.hansebooks.com**

DESIGN 127

A.P. CUTTING.
ARCHITECT.
WORCESTER. MASS.
SCALE ⅛ INCH TO 1 FOOT.

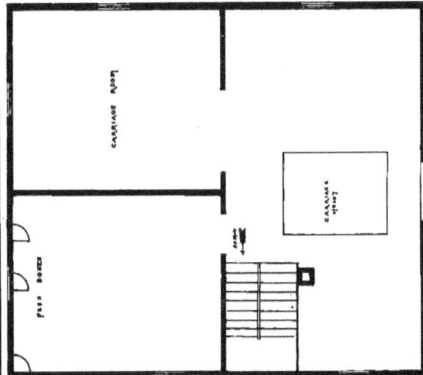

CARRIAGE ROOM

FEED BOXES

CARRIAGE WASH

PLAN OF SECOND FLOOR

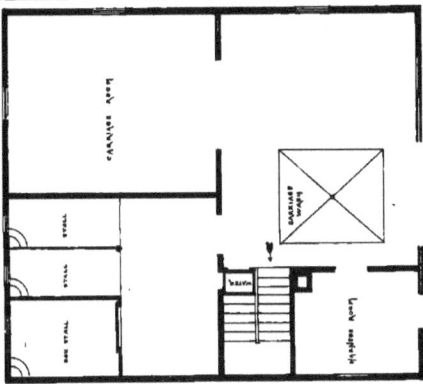

CARRIAGE ROOM

STALL

STALL

BOX STALL

HARNESS ROOM

HARNESS

DRESS

PLAN OF FIRST FLOOR

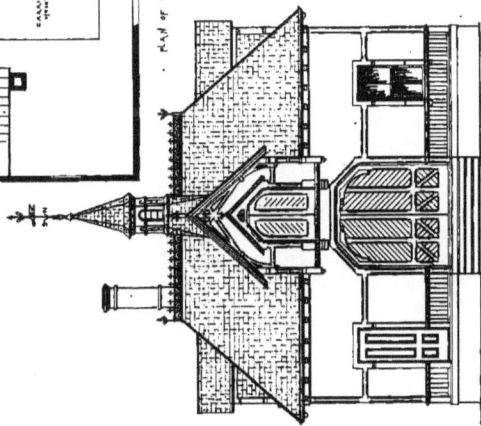

FRONT ELEVATION

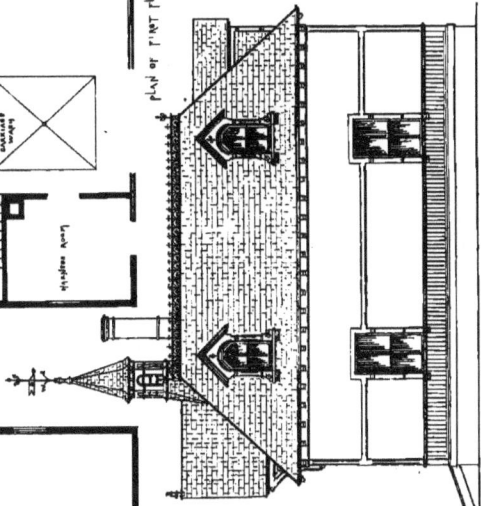

SIDE ELEVATION

HALF ELEVATION OF
DORMER WINDOW

FINIAL AT SUMMIT OF
HOOD OVER
HAY DOOR

ELEVATION OF
CUPOLA

SECTION OF OC.

SECTION OF COPPER
COVERED CUPOLA

SECTION OF
MAIN CORNICE

HALF ELEVATION OF
TWO PRINCIPAL DOOR

RIDGE CRESTING

SECTION OF CORNER BOARD

SECTION AT F.A.

SECTION AT A.

SECTION OF WINDOW JAMB

SECTION AT O.D.

PLAN OF CUPOLA

DETAILS OF STABLE FOR
F.A. WHITNEY,
LEOMINSTER, MASS.

A.P. CUTTING, ARCHITECT
WORCESTER, MASS.

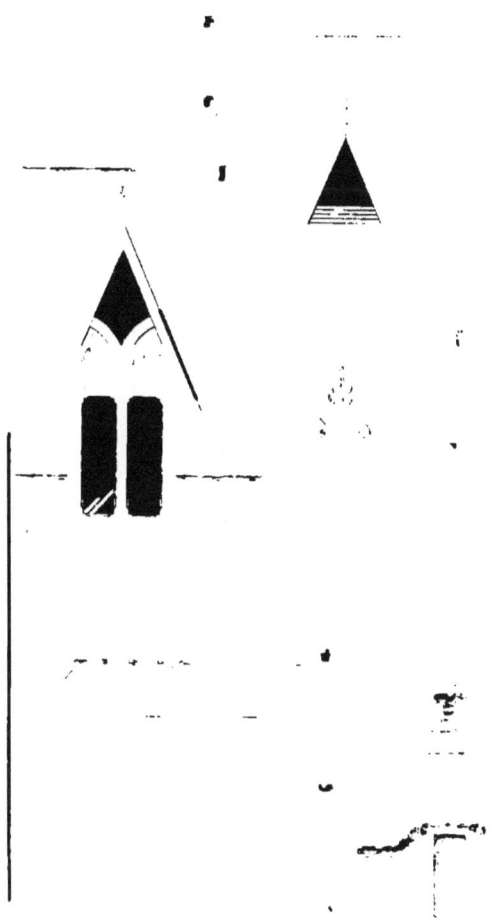

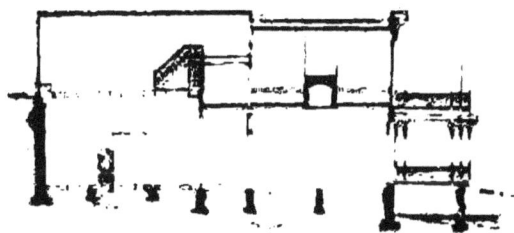

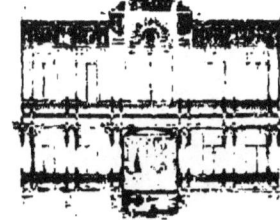

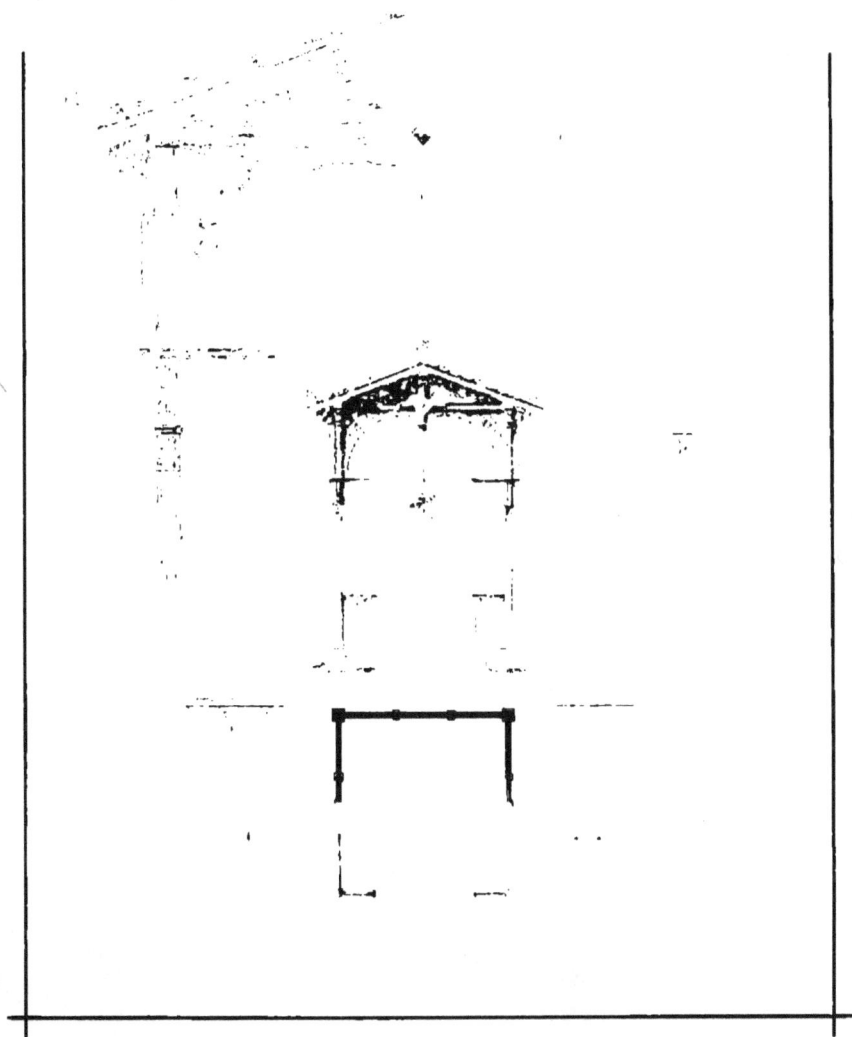

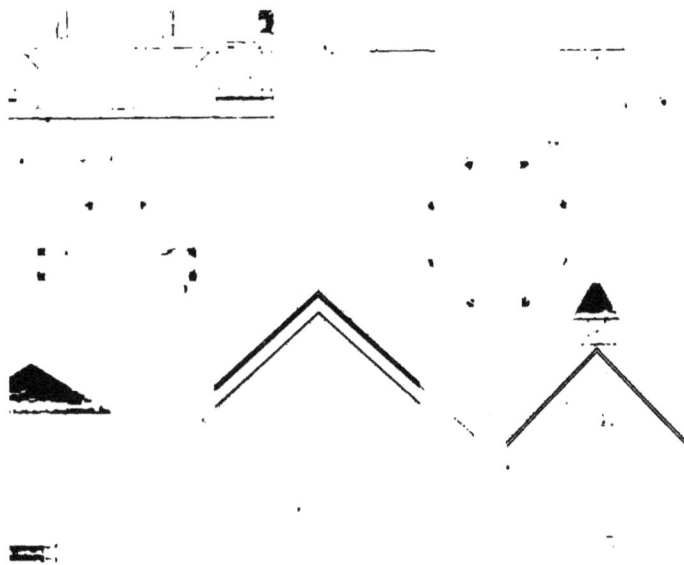

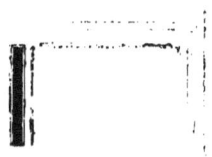

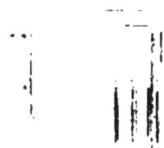

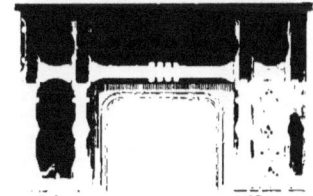

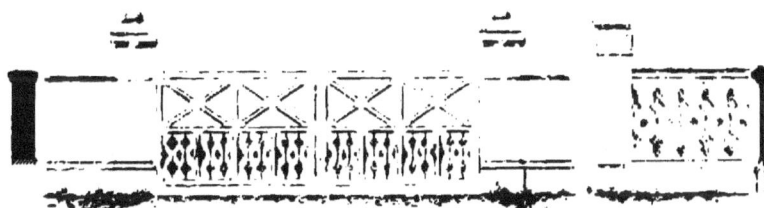

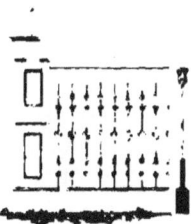

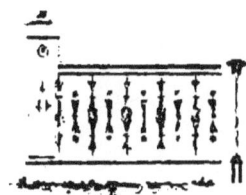

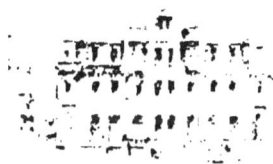

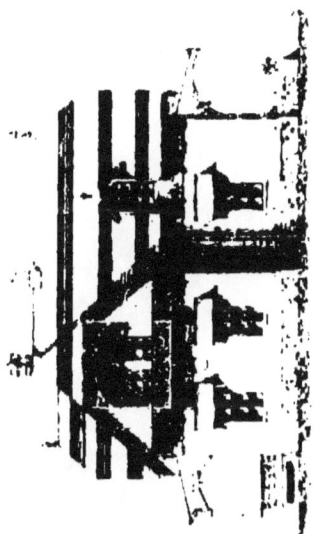

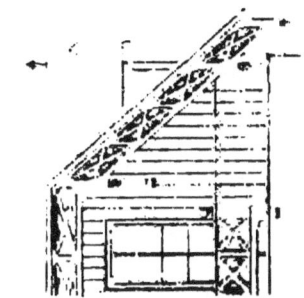

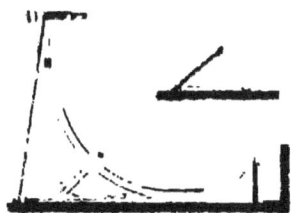

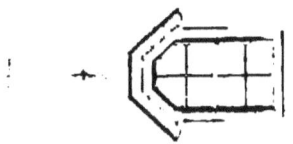

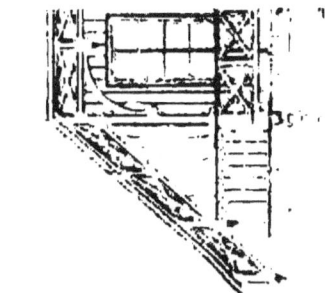

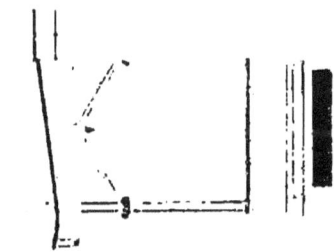

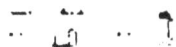

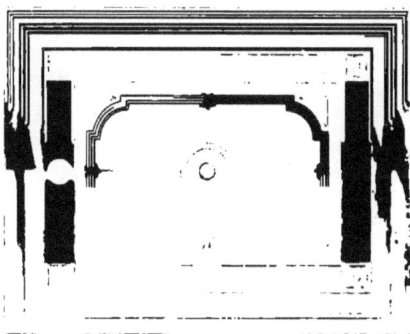

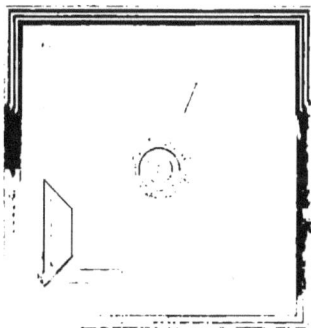

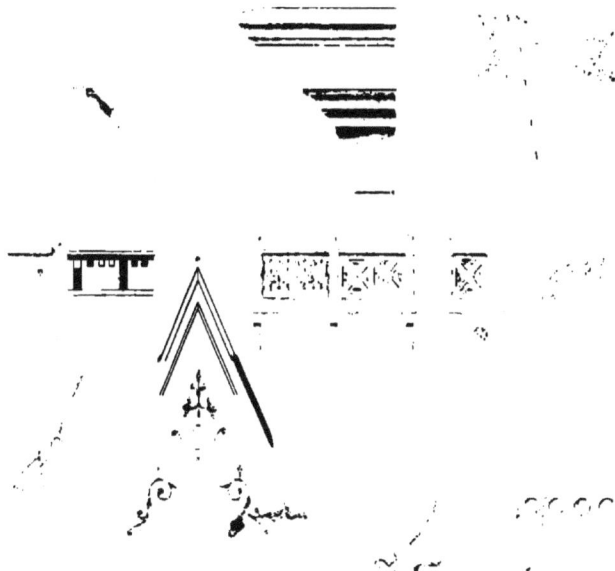

rules of 3

Brives

www.ingramcontent.com/pod-product-compliance
Lightning Source LLC
Chambersburg PA
CBHW021522090426
42739CB00007B/735